RODEO BARREL RACING

RODEO

Tex McLeese

he Rourke Press, Inc.

o Beach, Florida 32964

PHOTO CREDITS:
© Dennis K. Clark: pages 4, 7, 8, 10, 12, 13, 15, 17, 18; © Texas Department of Tourism: cover, title page; © Pro Rodeo Cowboy Association: page 21

EDITORIAL SERVICES:
Pamela Schroeder

Library of Congress Cataloging-in-Publication Data

McLeese, Tex, 1950-
   Rodeo barrel racing / Tex McLeese.
      p. cm. — (Rodeo discovery library)
   Includes index.
   ISBN 1-57103-347-5
   1. Barrel racing—Juvenile literature. [1. Barrel racing. 2. Rodeos.] I. Title.

GV1834.45.B35 M34 2000
791.8'4—dc21
                                        00–022624

TABLE OF CONTENTS

AN EVENT FOR WOMEN

Barrel racing (BARE ul RAY sing) is the one **rodeo** (ROW dee oh) event that is only for women. Girls who want to join the rodeo are allowed to compete in other events as well, but not many of them do. At least they don't compete in the same rodeo events as men. Some women who want to be calf ropers or bronc riders might ride in an all-women rodeo. However, those rodeos started to disappear with the rise of barrel racing. Today, almost all women in rodeo become barrel racers.

A grand entry for women riders.

WOMEN IN THE WILD WEST

Early in rodeo's history, cowgirls were more likely to compete against cowboys. From the late 1800s into the early 1900s, rodeos were usually local events. People who worked on ranches would try to show who the best ropers and riders were. In the Wild West shows that were also popular during that time, **Annie Oakley** (ANN ee OKE lee) was as famous as any cowboy. She was great at shooting a gun.

Cowgirls rode with cowboys in early rodeos.

TOO DANGEROUS?

By the 1930s, however, people thought the rodeo was too rough and dangerous for women. After a couple of female rodeo riders died in horse accidents, only men could compete. Protesters argued that rodeo could be dangerous for men as well as women. However, by the 1940s, the only rodeos that would allow females to compete were all-women rodeos.

Rodeos are still dangerous for women.

NATIONAL COWGIRL MUSEUM
AND
HALL OF FAME

RISE OF BARREL RACING

In the 1950s, barrel racing became a popular event for women. It took a lot of skill to ride a horse around the **barrels** (BARE ulz). However, it wasn't as dangerous as roping a steer or riding a bucking bull. Barrel races were held by the Girls Rodeo Association through the 1950s. By the late 1960s, many professional rodeos had barrel racing as the one event for women.

A barrel is put in place.

The art of barrel racing.

The horse leans into the barrel.

RULES OF BARREL RACING

This is a very fast event. The horse runs into the **arena** (uh REE nuh) at full **gallop** (GAL up). The horse and rider must race their way around three barrels in a pattern called a **cloverleaf** (CLO ver LEEF). The rider turns left past one barrel and right past another. Then the horse runs around the barrel at the furthest end of the arena and rushes back to the starting line.

The horse and rider use teamwork in barrel racing.

HITTING THE BARRELS

For a quick race, the riders go as close to the barrels as they can. The horse can touch or even move a barrel. However if it knocks one over, five seconds is added to the time. The winning time is usually less than 18 seconds. The difference between first and second place is often less than a tenth of a second.

The horse can touch or move a barrel.

BECOMING A BARREL RACER

The most important parts of barrel racing are being a good rider and having a good horse. The rider and horse must work very well together. Barrel racers own their horses. It can be expensive. A horse and trailer can easily cost more than $20,000. It is much cheaper for a bull or bronc rider to compete because the rodeo supplies the bucking animal.

A horse trailer can cost thousands of dollars.

HALL OF FAME HORSE

Some horses become as famous as their riders. "Scamper," a bay American **Quarter Horse** (KWOR tur HORS), won nine straight world championships for its rider, Charmayne James. Scamper joined the Pro Rodeo Hall of Fame in 1995. Charmayne James Rodman (she married rodeo roper Walt Rodman) has been rodeo's biggest female superstar. She was the first female to earn more than a million dollars from the sport.

Scamper won 9 straight World Championships with Charmayne Rodman.

THE WOMEN'S PROFESSIONAL RODEO ASSOCIATION

After barrel racing became an event for women to earn prize money at the biggest and most popular rodeos, the Girls Rodeo Association became the Women's Professional Rodeo Association. The WPRA had 3,000 members in 1975. However there were less than 1,500 members 20 years later. Still, rodeo is one of the few sports where a woman champion can earn as much as a man. Barrel racing is one of the rodeo's most popular events.

GLOSSARY

Annie Oakley (ANN ee OKE lee) — the most famous cowgirl of the Wild West

arena (uh REE nuh) — area where the rodeo takes place, either indoors or outdoors

barrel (BARE ul) — large container with curved sides and a flat top and bottom, usually metal in rodeos

barrel racing (BARE ul RAY sing) — a timed event in the rodeo for women on horseback

cloverleaf (CLO ver LEEF) — pattern made by the three barrels, which make the rider turn one way first, then the other way

gallop (GAL up) — the fast run of a horse

Quarter Horse (KWOR tur HORS) — American breed of saddle horse

rodeo (ROW dee oh) — a sport with events using the roping and riding skills that cowboys needed in the Old West

INDEX